Chasing The Devil Covid-19

MARK SUPERTRAMP MENDOZA

Fulton Books
Meadville, PA

Published by Fulton Books 2024

ISBN 979-8-89427-011-1 (paperback)
ISBN 979-8-89427-012-8 (digital)

Printed in the United States of America

Contents

Introduction

EVERYBODY SEEMS TO BE writing a book, so I figured what the hell. Doctors, scientists, politicians, and so on.

How will history be told about this pandemic now and in the future?

Every writer has a different view and style. Will they be honest or spin the reality of the pain and suffering?

I am no writer; I am just a person like the rest of you. Trying to survive.

We all lived it and felt its pain in so many ways, some lost loved ones, some lost livelihoods, some lived in fear, but we were all affected in some way.

History is about the past, but this chapter in history is not done yet. We can never predict the future, and it seems we have not learned from the past.

This journal is written as an observation of the tragic events that took place during the coronavirus pandemic. I will try to keep it objective, but there are some things I will have to point out. I want the reader to explore and think for themselves. "What did they hear and see during their time in lockdown?"

I am not a writer by any means, and I will be all over the place in this journal, but I will try to keep it as simple as possible. I am writing this for the people who lost loved ones during this crisis, but also for the brave men and women who battled this silent enemy. The title came from a health care worker in a nursing home where the virus took a deadly toll on the elderly who lived there. I will look at both sides and try to keep it logical, not too political. There are two sides to every story, and then there is the truth. That is always the million-dollar question.

In the Beginning

WHEN THE CORONAVIRUS HIT the USA, it started out small, but it soon spread like wildfire from state to state. The virus had already started taking its toll in other countries around the world with death and the fear of being infected. The whole world was going on lockdown, and the medical field was in a race to find a cure to save lives.

Hospitals were overwhelmed and pushing the limits, supplies were running low in every country except one. Every leader was asking for help and just trying to keep up with the crisis. It was an unknown disease, and uncertainty is the greatest power fear has in life.

New York City was hit hard in the beginning and suffered great losses. The health care personnel pushed through the chaos, day after day, putting their own lives at risk to save others. All over the world, brave men and women were at risk but stood strong against an invisible enemy.

Every state had a different number of cases and was dealing with the virus in different ways. The elderly were the most vulnerable and those with certain health issues according to the data. Some state leaders were just really lost, and it became more about politics. Leaders who had nothing to lose threatened people who had everything to lose.

As the coronavirus spread, it was difficult to understand the experts because no one knew anything about the virus; it was a learn-as-you-go situation. The public was told that masks were not needed by Dr. F, and then it changed weeks later to say that they were needed.

The World Health Organization was no better in their information and kept flip-flopping through this whole ordeal. The only country that knew anything was not talking to anyone, not even the WHO. The organization that is supposed to be the one entrusted to notify the world of dangerous diseases and outbreaks around the world, so the world thought?

We were told that the lockdowns were needed to flatten the curve and not overwhelm the hospitals in the beginning, and that all would change as the cases and death toll began to rise.

We are in the month of January as I begin this journal.

THE WIZARD

I did a little digging on the internet and found out that one of the first cases came from a gentleman who had traveled to Wuhan, China, and returned to the USA on January 15, 2020. On January 20, 2020, he tested positive for the virus.

The doctors started treating the patient, but the unknown is always hard to figure out. It is a guessing game, but on day seven, they give him a drug called Remdesivir, which seems to help his condition. The article I found ends with the patient still in the hospital but doesn't give a conclusion. He is thirty-five years old and in decent health, which gives me hope that he made it through and is okay.

I keep watching this crisis continue on the news, and on January 28, 2020, the president blocks flights from China, which shows me that he has been notified of the situation.

We know what happens next, so it's not worth repeating, but just in case you missed it, some people lost their minds!

We see the experts on TV, and they are optimistic that we will be okay. You even had certain politicians saying the same thing. It's going to be alright, go out and live your life. Everybody seems to be on the same page for now, do not panic.

The president is being impeached currently, but he is still trying to do his job.

We are coming into February, and things are beginning to change here and around the world as cases are growing. "America is going to begin locking down soon is the story, but when is the question?"

People are hitting the stores preparing for the worst, buying everything they will need to make it through the lockdowns. Cleaning supplies, toilet paper, wet wipes, food, etc. You name it, and it was flying off the shelves.

The CDC is giving out guidelines to all the states and starting to tell us the dos and don'ts as this virus continues to spread.

Everybody has the information, and it is up to them to make the call on the ground.

One governor blames the federal government and God for deaths in his state. When it's his order that puts older people with COVID-19 back into nursing homes. Instead of taking some responsibility for his own actions, he blames others for his incompetence! **Talk about having no shame!**

A governor oversees the state and has great power. What comes with great power?

A. Emmy
B. A book deal
C. Responsibility

On February 15, 2020, the worst governor in the world has a press conference. Trying to explain away his mistake and still blaming others, from the delivery guy to the nursing staff.

This governor also signed an order that would not hold nursing homes responsible for any deaths or government officials involved.

An aide to this guy even admitted to downplaying the number of people who passed away because she worried the Trump Department of Justice would investigate.

Why worry if you have nothing to hide?

It gets even worse when it is reported that this same guy is threatening retribution against a democratic congressman for asking questions on the matter.

On February 18, 2020, this same governor comes out and starts talking about voids. How he should have done more to combat disinformation and lies.

Void this and void that, spews the Godfather of Doom.

This governor still thinks he did nothing wrong, and most of the media agree. This guy was praised by so many people, but this conference was only on two cable stations.

I surfed the channels to see if there was more coverage, but nothing else on their hero. This governor's story is not over yet—to be continued!

A few governors made the same deadly mistake, but no one has covered their story. I challenge the reader to look into it for themselves.

Let's go to March 11, 2020, and it's being reported that there are 939 cases in the USA now. The lockdowns begin on March 21, 2020, with states and local leaders setting up their own restrictions according to what is happening on the ground and then notifying the federal government of their needs.

Pop-up facilities are being set up to handle the overflow from the hospitals, plus two medical ships are sent to New York and California to help in the effort.

During this time, it is being reported that a medication used for malaria and lupus is being used to treat people who have been infected with the coronavirus. Hydroxychloroquine plus a z-pack or zinc combo is being prescribed by some doctors around the world. It is also being reported that it can help people in the early stages before the virus gets worse.

Why do I bring this up? I will explain!

This drug has been around for decades and is being used on the unknown, but it is helping some people recover before they end up in intensive care. Some doctors refer to the result as inconclusive, but if it helps, why not use it? **I am no doctor, but it seems logical if you have nothing else in your toolbox.**

The president brings it up as a positive thing, but the mainstream media, some doctors, and social media turn it into a negative thing, and before you know it, this medication is on a no-use list.

The media and certain doctors are saying that hydroxychloroquine is affecting the heart and should not be prescribed to patients anymore. No one stopped to think that maybe the vaccines could be affecting the heart or even the virus itself. It does attack the lungs after all, so why not the heart? But we will never know because no one really cares in doom and gloom land. **It was all hydroxychloroquine; no more for you.**

The only answer at this time is to wear a mask, wash your hands, social distance and stay home unless you are an essential worker.

Doctors who continue to help patients with this combo are threatened and vilified. People in the media who believe in this treatment are met with the same. A drug that can help someone is better than going into the ICU any day, you would think?

On April 14, 2020, Congresswoman KW from Michigan thanked the president for basically saving her life. She took hydroxychloroquine because she was having trouble breathing and survived her ordeal. Which is great news, but thanking the president is not allowed, period.

On April 23, 2020, she is censured by the Democratic Party and is not allowed to speak about her experience anymore. KW said she would not be silenced by her peers, but that was not the case. She had only spoken out a few times, and that was enough to shut her down. On April 24, 2020, a person called J. Shaw posted, "We own her." **What kind of person would say this about another human being?**

Hydroxychloroquine would have a bad rap from here on out, and it is only April. Four weeks, not fifteen days, into this lockdown with no vaccine yet.

In a time of great need, politics and the unknown collide. "A crisis should never go to waste," I hear some leaders say out loud. We have an opportunity to make the changes we want in society!

While so many people are suffering, this is the mindset of our so-called leaders. Let's take advantage of this misery and pain so we can get our agenda through.

Operation Warp Speed has been put together. It's a partnership between the drug companies and the federal government to work on a vaccine in record time.

Some say it's impossible, but we will see what happens.

When you have hope, nothing is impossible!

Rolling into May, it becomes clear that these lockdowns are going to continue. Congress has passed a mass spending bill to help the American people who are suffering financially, but as usual, they add crap to it that has nothing to do with relief.

The bill is signed by the president, and the money goes out to the American people.

In June, the powers that be were still fighting over what to do next. You have politicians not following their own lockdown rules and still punishing people who are hanging on by a thread.

Talk about how not to lead in a crisis!

The Good, the Bad and the Worst

Let's start with the doctors, nurses, first responders, and all the people who kept this country going while under tremendous pressure and great sacrifice. While so many of us were locked up in our homes, these people were still working.

You saw so many people trying to help where they could and figuring out ways to make it through this crisis. One story reported a person leaving a $1200 tip at a restaurant and the owner splitting it up between his employees. A man in New Orleans was letting his customers run a tab for groceries and needed supplies. DP of Barstool Sports started a GoFundMe for restaurants in need, which has saved many local eateries. **Let's not forget the children**: the little girl who made bracelets to sell, the boy who ran around his yard to raise money—the heart of a child is a wonderful thing. People who just cared and wanted to help a neighbor, stranger, or friend. I know there are more great stories out there that I didn't see or hear about, but maybe you did. **A small act of kindness can go a long way during tough times. It can mean so much in a time of need.**

Unfortunately, most of the media does not fall into that box. In the past, there were actual reporters who went out and investigated their own stories and searched for the truth, period! There was no left, right, or in between—just the truth. The media dismissed any signs of hope because of their bias toward this president. Some of their guest doctors also jumped on the doom and gloom wagon. **If all doctors were perfect, there would not be a show called** Botched!

There was a story of a ninety-year-old woman who survived cancer and COVID-19. It should have been a heartfelt story, but leave it to the reporter to mess it up. Turning it into a political opposition piece. An uplifting story about survival shot to hell. Thanks, crappy media!

Hollywood was not any better with actors, talk show hosts, and comedians lecturing people from their million-dollar mansions. Hollywood lives in a bubble of decadence, not in the real world, and that's fine, but to lecture people who don't have millions of dollars and are hurting is pretty ridiculous. Talk shows became toxic and hate-filled, and late night wasn't funny anymore like Johnny Carson or Jay Leno. Hollywood just lost all its imagination and humor. It has become politically correct, which kills imagination and humor. Look at the old TV shows turned into movies, comic books coming to life, and reboots of TV classics.

Now we come to the master deceivers, politicians who took advantage and abused their power in a time of pain. This is where I won't hold back because these are the people that are supposed to be watching out for our country in good and bad times. Career liars who got rich selling out America for decades, getting richer while Americans got poorer.

Most of the members of Congress have been there for way too long and have forgotten their purpose when they put their hand on the Bible and took an oath to the Constitution. "You can't protect a country you do not believe in."

Some governors and mayors were just as bad as Congress. People that took an oath to defend the Constitution are ripping it to shreds by their actions. It's above my pay grade, PM explained to a TV host. This is a person in charge of a city, and this was his answer. Most of our leaders have forgotten that it is not about them or a certain party; it is about America, our home. I almost forgot about the mainstream media with 24/7 doom and gloom coverage. Talk about no-hope news and fear factors. I had to stop watching a lot of the news for a few days because it was so depressing.

Any kind of hope was quickly shut down by so many people in the media, it was shocking to see. It was an endless sea of misery 24/7 on some of these networks.

When President Trump came out and said, "Don't let this virus control you, and not to give up!" You would think some positivity would be well received, but no chance. If it had been someone else in the office, the reaction would have been different. **Ass-kissing all around!**

Social media shuts down any free thought or different opinion about the virus. Doctors who were treating patients with therapeutics that could help people were shut down. "Misinformation, they cried, as saviors of the internet and the world!"

Social media is okay but does the average person really need it?

Call the ones you love, write them a letter, send them a card, spend time with them if you can. I think they would love that more.

The owners of these companies do not care about you; all they care about is money and power. It's like smoking, drugs, or drinking; the choice is yours.

Get off the screen and send love the old-fashion way! The world will be a better place for it!

Essential Versus Nonessential?

S OME STATE LEADERS WERE not cut out to be in power, and you could tell by how they picked the essential and nonessential workers. We had weed shops, liquor stores, and even a drive-through strip club in one state open for business, but churches, restaurants, and so many other businesses were ordered to stay closed.

I talked to a few business owners, and the government was micromanaging them to death. You can do this, but you can't do that. Big box stores were allowed to stay open, but small businesses were going out of business.

Every business I talked to had gone the extra mile, and here they were getting hit again by our government. Egos, power trips, plus a pure hatred for this president were costing lives, and so much more.

These are the people that we count on to keep us safe and have some kind of common sense, but so many of them failed.

We had mayors punishing people for just trying to open their businesses; let's fine or take away their business license. Governors who sent the elderly back into nursing homes after testing positive for the virus. A judge even sent a hair salon owner to jail for not abiding by the rules in Texas. The judge wanted an admission of guilt and an ass kissing but she did not back down. She spent a day and a half in jail before the Lt. Governor intervened.

Essential vs. nonessential has been the messed up question since this whole thing started.

Let's follow the science, but everyone has a different answer because it's a new virus, so no one really knows the answers except the doctors in China.

Some people wanted a national plan, but would that have worked or been more damaging in so many different ways? Other countries tried a nationwide strict lockdown, and they still got hit again by the virus. Cases rose because locking up only delayed the inevitable, and some of these countries were going for it a second time, even if it cost people their livelihoods.

A restaurant owner in Los Angeles posted her emotional video on YouTube to the governor of California and the mayor of Los Angeles when a movie company was allowed to set up outdoor catering just a few feet away from her business, which had been shut down for months. Outdoor dining was keeping these businesses alive by a thread, and to shut them down again but allow a rich movie company to do as they please is definitely a slap in the face. It should show you that the people running these cities and states have no business in government.

The LA mayor's response was that his heart goes out to the owner, but the order stands. The governor followed suit after he was caught eating indoors with a bunch of people with no masks and no social distancing. No more outdoor dining in the State of California period. Take-out and delivery only.

I don't want to forget the gym owners who put up with the same power-hungry politicians who were fining them for trying to survive. In New Jersey, Atlias Gym had their finances taken from them by the state in the dark of night. The government had confiscated their funds while still going through the court case, just like that.

Are these the people we are supposed to trust?

You would think that trying to stay in shape would be a good idea, but I guess smoking weed and drinking beer are more essential for your health than trying to be fit.

I thought doctors were supposed to promote healthy living, but I guess I was wrong. Let's light one up and toss back a few, for health is the new prescription.

The churches being shut down were probably the hardest pill to swallow because they are protected and provide a needed service to so many people.

Churches big and small were being targeted all over the country by governors and mayors. People couldn't worship together or have a funeral service for a loved one unless permission was granted by your kings and queens of government. Churches had limits placed on them for capacity, and no singing was allowed by order of the king and queens.

On March 18, 2021, a Canadian preacher was put in prison for preaching in his church. Not following guidelines was his crime.

When people need hope, leaders arrest preachers! **The world is definitely hitting rock bottom!**

Our leaders have nothing to lose as far as money is concerned; they are considered essential, but what about you? What about your life? What about your freedom? What about your family?

Who is essential in the end?

The President Versus COVID-19

On October 1, 2020, the president and the first lady tested positive for the virus. The next day, he was flown to Walter Reed Medical Center to start treatment. It was reported that he was given a medical cocktail of drugs and was going to be given some experimental treatment dealing with antibodies.

It did not take long for the media and the haters to start up the cruel attacks.

A few days later, the president was doing better and was going back to the White House, not a 100 percent, but okay. You would think this would be good news, but it wasn't; the hate continued.

"What does this say about our society today?"

Many people in the White House tested positive for the virus and were taking appropriate measures. The president continued his treatment, and within ten days he seemed to be his old self, which drove the media nuts. The first lady took a little longer, but she also recovered, which was good news too!

We hear about tolerance from a lot of these so-called tolerant people, and it's a joke. We will call them self-righteous sinners because it is all about selfishness and hate when you wish harm on another human being. "What kind of messed up person wishes death or illness on someone who's sick?"

"Mr. DL wondered why the president didn't take hydroxychloroquine at the time of his illness."

I will take a logical guess, Mr. DL—that his age and his condition played a role in the treatment he was given by his doctors.

COVID-19 has taken so many lives, and it should have been a team effort from the start, but hate blinded our country, so when it came, we were not prepared to take it on as needed.

Our leaders were fighting over 2016, phone calls, and a dossier. Any solution offered or presented by the president or different doctors other than Dr. F were quickly dismissed. Let's follow the science I kept hearing, or this is not science-based.

When you have an emergency and lives are on the line, you never take anything off the table!

Remember, there is still no vaccine at this time, but it's in the works.

It's almost November 3, 2020, and a vaccine is in the final testing stage and waiting for emergency authorization.

The vaccine is soon to be cleared for emergency use, and distribution to the states has begun. Which is great news, and a second vaccine is about to be cleared too!

Deep Thought

THROUGH THIS WHOLE CRISIS, every state ran their own corona task force in way. Some states were good, and some states were bad, but all were trying to save lives in their own way. I gave them that much credit in the beginning, but unfortunately, as weeks turned into months, it became clear that so many of our leaders used this tragedy to push through an agenda. It became more about power, egos, and, in the end, trying to get President Trump out of office.

I heard governors and mayors blame the people for the rise in cases. This is your fault, so we will shut down again until you obey.

I want the reader to really look at what took place and what decisions were made by different politicians and leaders. "Did they truly follow the science, or did they take advantage of the crisis?"

Americans received financial help in late May and July, but gridlock in Congress was about to get worse. Because there was an election coming up in November, you were out of luck for any further relief until the bad orange man was out of office.

This was admitted by NP after the 2020 election was all done.

Americans had to suffer for months because politicians could not let go of their hate, and so many people paid the price.

Hate destroys everything it touches; unfortunately, we have too many haters in charge of this country.

Politicians who have been in power for decades, despite the damage they do and have done during this crisis. It was business as usual for the swamp, even in an emergency.

The one thing I noticed during this crisis is that no real light was shed on treatment in hospitals. People were going into hospitals and getting out, but there was no true coverage of how patients were being treated.

I saw oxygen and other things being done to patients, but no treatment explanation. Nothing from the CDC or WHO; nothing on local news or mainstream news. President Trump was covered when he got the virus, but no other real coverage of how people were surviving this nightmare. I saw some survival stories, but still no answers on how they were treated. Most of the coverage is about the rise in cases and the unvaccinated now.

The Holidays and COVID-19

THE HOLIDAYS WERE DIFFERENT in the year of COVID-19 and probably will be for some time, but people still need to have some kind of life. Holidays are meant to be spent with family and friends, not with lockdowns and fear. Everyone knows the guidelines by now, and no expert has truly connected the dots as to where someone catches the virus. One day you can have no signs, and the next day you are sick.

It's almost Thanksgiving, and the government is still telling people how to celebrate with their families while the California governor breaks his own rules, imposing a curfew in California beginning Saturday, November 21, 2020. In my opinion, he is just mad because he got caught and is punishing the people of California. What a guy?

Its December 6, 2020, and I now have my answer for Christmas from the governor of California: there will be a new shutdown of all nonessential businesses in California, and the mayor of Los Angeles is canceling Christmas for all of the city residents—no Christmas for you! The governor is telling people to limit the number of guests in their own home, and if you don't, we can punish you.

It is December 13, 2020, and GN has locked down California again for three weeks because the beds are at capacity in many places in the state.

It will be a new year when I start this part of the journal again.

New Year 2021 and a New President

THERE IS A NEW administration that is going to have to continue the fight against COVID-19. Let's see how they will handle this situation.

It's January 31, 2021, and this administration is writing executive orders at a record pace. Only a few orders deal with the pandemic, and Congress is still trying to get a relief bill deal done.

California is slowly opening up, but with micromanagement by the government once again. There is a recall of the king of California, who loves to preach but does not practice what he preaches. Politicians have been forcing people to give up their freedom while they break their own rules!

It is February 7, 2021, and this administration has offered up stadiums for vaccine distribution, plus pharmacies are going to start giving out shots too. The last administration had pharmacies in their plan, but stadiums were not offered until after the 2020 election.

The problem for both presidents was supply! The whole world is in need, but not enough to go around yet.

A lot of decisions are still being left up to the states because they know the needs of their people. MAYBE? Congress is still… working on a relief bill with a bunch of unrelated stuff in it, but it will go through because that's what politicians do!

"Talk about adding salt to a wound!"

It is February 21, 2021, and the pandemic is still not over, but some states are open for business.

These are the free states of America and are dealing with the pandemic in a different way.

On March 13, 2021, President Biden addresses the nation about the virus, asking the people of America to keep doing the basic three things we have been doing for the last year. President Biden adds that if we do as he asked, we might be able to have small gatherings by July 4, 2021.

It's in March that Congress passes a relief bill. **The relief bill tour will soon follow. Talk about a government gone bad!**

If you have to go out and explain a so-called relief bill, it's a con job.

Remember the NP line from the past about the healthcare bill.

Politicians are some of the biggest con artists in the world! I have to give them credit.

We are ending March 2021 with more vaccines being given out, and the president is about to make more people eligible to get the shot.

The sad thing is that he is also letting thousands of people across the border with a 10 percent COVID-19 rate, and those are just the ones we know of, which makes no sense during a pandemic.

I thought a president was supposed to protect his country.

California is starting to open up more, and you are seeing the king come out and make appearances. A June 15, 2021, full open date is the word from the king, as long as the numbers are good.

It is April 2021, and I am sad to see the Easter bunny in a mask at the JP briefing. Sure, just keep the doom and gloom going for the country.

You had the presidents and the CDC person come out and literally say she was scared on national TV.

Talk about the party of no hope.
The world is hurting, and this is the message from America.
We are still in April, and President B. has a message for the American people. Two hundred million people have been vaccinated in the USA, which is good news, but there is still a long way to go.

At the end of April, President Biden comes out with new vaccine numbers for Americans and is asked a question about India, which is seeing more deaths and cases grow. President Biden's response is that we are sending aid, including **Remdesivir,** to India.

Think about that answer for a minute.

America is sending Remdesivir to help with COVID-19 in another country.

I thought we had nothing in the toolbox; this is what I kept hearing from these people.

It was all about the vaccine!
The shots have stalled a little, so we now have politicians, celebrities, and doctors all out in force trying to get people to get vaccinated. Dishing out money, food, and other prizes just to get you to take the vaccine. These are some of the same people that were talking negatively about the vaccine before it was cleared for emergency use. It couldn't be done in less than a year, or I am not taking it if President Trump says it's okay to take it. Funny how all the naysayers were the first to jump in line to get a shot they didn't believe in months ago. There is a lot of doubt and fear in the minds of many Americans.

Mask or not mask? Vaccine or not to vaccine?
The Biden administration has left it up to the businesses to take charge of how they will handle COVID-19 issues in their establishments. **Right?** The federal government has talked about COVID-19 passports, and so have some states politicians.

Is it right to force people to take a vaccine or have a medical passport to live life?
If you look back in history, has this been done before, and under what circumstances? Were people forced to give up their freedom because the people in charge forced them to?

Power corrupts many people, and you can hear it being said out loud by the politicians.

People still have questions and concerns about the vaccine, and that should be okay, you would think? When you are sick, what do you usually do?

A.   Go to the doctor to get checked out.
B.   Take some over-the-counter medicine.
C.   Get a shot.
D.   Let your condition heal on its own, a.k.a. the common cold.

Everybody has different bodies and health issues; one size does not fit all! **The seeds of doubt** were sewn early by politicians, doctors, the media, and social media, so they have no one to blame for hesitation and fear but themselves!

There will be no self-reflection by any of these people because it is not in them. Control and power—that's all they crave.

On May 13, 2021, President Biden makes the announcement that if you have been vaccinated, you no longer need to wear a mask, but if not, you can still mask up until you get the vaccine. The CDC still has the same message, but with a little warning about indoor activities. Outside mask wearing is off the table too, but some leaders are still holding on to the mask.

One couple in Florida was arrested for letting people in their gym with no mask. The governor of Florida helps them out and has said that anyone who has been treated in this manner can report it to his office.

Getting arrested in America for not wearing a mask. I think the police have more important work to do than arresting people who are not wearing masks.

America is not the only place this has been happening. I challenge the reader to explore where else in the world this is going on.

It's June 2021, and President Biden declares a national month of action to get more vaccines into the arms of Americans who have still not taken the vaccine.

It's June 15, 2021, and the king of California is opening up the state with little restrictions. It will be up to businesses to handle their customers and employees now. New York is even easing back on restrictions along with some other states, but some states are still below vaccine levels, which means government restrictions are still in place. It's July 7, 2021, and things are still not well with two variants that are causing COVID-19 cases to rise. Dr. F has been out telling people to get vaccinated because the new variants spreading are more contagious. President Biden has an idea about going door-to-door giving out information on the vaccines. It's July 13, 2021, and I spot this on the news. The king of California and the mayor of New York are mandating masks in classrooms for kids who are not vaccinated. Teachers do not have to wear a masks if vaccinated, and the kids can play outside without a mask. How gracious of them?

I thought we were following science, and kids that are infected can recover if they do not have underlying conditions.

An adult would give the child a choice, especially if that adult was vaccinated!

Instead, we are mandating, a.k.a. forcing kids to wear them. You had a teacher yelling at a high school student who had his vaccine and was not wearing a mask in class. The student sat there calm and cool while she screamed at him.

This person is teaching your kids. Wow!

Later that day, I saw doctor get over it push for vaccine mandates. We all know that a lot of politicians love government mandates and are pawning off mandates to employers to get around the Constitution and laws that protect us from an overreaching government.

Now, the Biden DOJ has proven my point.

Vaccines are legal to mandate, according to MG. This DOJ is also dropping the investigation into the nursing home tragedy in New York City.

Talk about a government, not for the people.

A DOJ that turns its back on the Constitution and the rule of law.

It's July 27, 2021, and I am seeing protests break out in other countries. Germany is having people arrested for protesting the lockdowns.

Australia has helicopter flying around its beaches, telling citizens to go home or face a fine.

The people are tired and wanting some kind of freedom back, but the people in charge are not listening.

It's August 3, 2021, and I see CC on TV talking about how selfish you are if you do not get vaccinated. This is the same guy who was out riding his bike when he was supposed to be in quarantine for 14 days. Luckily, some guy recorded the encounter, for hypocrisy's sake. You probably did not hear about it because most of the media sucks, and it was last year when he got caught. **Old news, same dude. You are selfish, and do not forget it**. It's August 9, 2021, when I saw this report on the news. Police are checking for vaccine status at cafes in France. Talk about kings and queens in power.

The shocking thing is America is on the same path and doctor get over it is cool with it.

The military will be forcing its troops to get the vaccine, and the unvaccinated will follow.

President Biden is pushing the FDA to fully approve the vaccines, and that will be it for those who do not want to receive the vaccine.

Kids, Teachers and COVID-19

I HAVE GREAT RESPECT FOR teachers, but after seeing a math teacher on the news on March 1, 2021, traveling around the USA, and going to every In-N-Out burger joint for the past few months, I was pissed.

Kids are struggling all over this country, and this teacher is out with his family on a mission to hit every In-N-Out burger place in the USA.

You had another teacher posting pictures of herself on vacation at the beach.

You had board members talking crap about how parents want their babysitters back. **Teachers are not babysitters; it is your job. If you do not like it, find another job!**

The teachers' union is a party all to themselves, and they're making all kinds of demands before they go back to work. Some reasonable but most outrageous, having nothing to do with teaching your kids or getting back to school.

It is March 3, 2021, and a lot of the kids are still out of class around this country. So many of them are hurting, but the unions have a hold on our politicians. You have all first responders, city workers, and others in public services who are still working. They have been working through this whole crisis; how do I know because I have friends who are first responders.

I have seen stories about suicide and depression dealing with children, but the unions need more money in the schools to make them safe.

Let's be brutally honest: teachers are all still getting paid to do Zoom classes but refuse to go back to in-door learning until their demands are met.

On March 15, 2021, it was reported that some teacher unions want bonuses for themselves from the so-called relief package. It's basically getting a raise while your kids are not in class.

What a betrayal of what a teacher used to be in this country!

I remember parents having a say in their child's education, not the unions—the original PTA, where parents of the school were involved and informed on their child's progress.

My mom and dad were in the PTA at my school when I was a kid. A small group of parents and teachers working together as a team. When parents have more say, it makes a big difference in a child's education.

Parents need to take back the schools because these are your kids.

The children would be better off without unions, committees, boards, councils, and even the Department of Education. All you need are loving parents who are involved in their kids' education and teachers who do not have agendas. Teachers who are there to teach their subject: math, science, reading, and nothing more. Our public schools have been failing the children for years, and unfortunately, this crisis has shown us the reason why!

I talked to a teacher who can communicate straight to the principal of her school with any problems she encounters. **This school district is not part of a union.**

She says it works because there is no union to deal with, just the child, parents, principal, and teacher.

The union thinks these children belong to them, but these are your kids; you are the mother and father, not a union or a teacher.

I remember a time when a teacher taught for the love of teaching, not an agenda.

I had many teachers who were awesome and pushed me to do my best. A mom and dad who always believed in me even when I didn't believe in myself.

Sometimes, it's that simple when it comes to your kids! You should be the main teacher in their life, not the unions or government.

It's May 21, 2021, and I just saw two reports on kids talking to their district school boards about wearing masks in school. It was really cool to see because what is happening to the children is not right! Studies early on showed that kids were not big carriers, and if they did become ill, they would be able to fight it off better than older people.

These two children asked the school board, "Why do I have to wear a mask when I am outside playing?" Did the school board care? Probably not, but it was awesome to see a child have more sense than a grownup.

The teacher's union demands that all children be vaccinated before returning to school. Who is in charge of public schools today?

Unions of the past used to serve a purpose, but today, they really do not. The union acts like these kids belong to them, but they are your children.

If a teacher wants to screw up their kid on their own time, that's their business, but once in the classroom, it becomes your business. Teachers are supposed to serve the public, not themselves.

Teachers are essential, but the unions, boards, committees, and all the rest are not really needed if it is truly about the children. It's like big government too much is not a good thing.

Speaking of big government, the Los Angeles school district in California gave a fourth-grade child the vaccine without the parent's consent. The person told the child not to tell his mother and gave him a slice of pizza as a reward. A child is told by a stranger to lie to his own mother!

Who in the hell do these people think they are? Her child has health issues, and to have some stranger put her child at risk is criminal! These are not your kids; you did not give birth to them.

If you want to teach, then do so; if you are scared, protect yourself, but leave the children alone!

It has been two years, and I have been waiting for a teacher to stand up for the children and mean it. It finally happened in January

2022. I see this teacher who has cancer and is teaching the kids. He has had enough of the union and just wants to teach. That is his passion, COVID-19 or cancer; he wants to teach. Imagine a teacher who wants to teach and is essential to a young mind, who has the courage to stand up to the goliath, a.k.a. the union.

I am sure there are more teachers out there like this man, but "they are far and in between."

I will end with this note: a child is born innocent; a child is born fearless; a child is born with hopes and dreams. It is up to the parents to teach their children about life. A teacher's job is to provide them with the basic tools to help them in life.

Fear or Freedom?

A president once said," The only thing we have to fear is fear itself!"

Some people might know who this president was, and some may not. **Take a look and see who he was and the struggles of his time.**

Fear is a powerful emotion, and everybody has their fears in life. "How do we overcome them is always the challenge."

It is March 7, 2021, and we have come back around to the beginning of the lockdowns. A year of pain and sadness for so many people around the world. The virus continues, but we now have three vaccines being distributed as fast as possible.

When it comes to using fear, politicians sure got it down. Using fear, hate, anger, and lies to gain power and control over people is the name of the game. When people are kept in a constant state of emotion instead of logic, it is easy to divide them.

You have people being threatened for not wearing a mask by strangers. You had a sixty-seven-year-old lady get arrested in a bank for not wearing a mask in Texas.

We are a year into this pandemic, and some of the people in charge seem like they don't want it to end. It's like we are hamsters on a spinning wheel.

Dr. F keeps going out on networks and scaring the shit out of people. The truth is, no one knows everything about this virus except China. Anybody can sit behind a desk and read reports; it's a whole lot different when you're treating patients.

The host, AC, on one of the networks, said that fear is a good thing.

This is true to a point, but when that fear cripples you from living your life or giving up your freedom, that's not a good thing.

If people were afraid all the time, we wouldn't have police, firemen, soldiers, etc. Dreams would never come true in life if we were always afraid.

Some people can control their fear better than others, and this is what makes them different. Most people run away from danger, but these people run toward it.

Think about all the jobs out there that are risky or would be hard to do if you were always afraid!

Doctors, nurses, police, firefighters, paramedics, EMTs, and so many more. What is your dream, and are you going to let fear stop you?

Politicians use fear because it's easy to scare people into submission and to give up their freedom.

Remember, in Monsters Inc., they used fear to power their world. "Guess who the monsters are today?"

Let's talk about freedom and how precious it is. You have countries around the world that do not have the freedoms that America has, but we joined the world in lockdowns because that's what the experts said to do.

It was only supposed to be fifteen days.

A year later, we are trying to get our freedom back, trying to live our lives like we did before the pandemic hit, but you have some people who do not want to go back to the way it was before. The vultures of the world who only want power and control.

Vulture: A rapacious or predatory person or a person who tries to take advantage of someone who is in a bad situation.

We the People

These people see an opportunity to take advantage of this tragedy. Talking about virus passports and other measures to keep an eye on people.

This is happening in the Land of the Free and Home of the Brave!

It has been said that freedom isn't free!

Who wrote it? Look it up for yourselves and see.

Think about freedom and liberty!

What America stands for!

Most of all, think about the sacrifices made by those who paid the ultimate price for our freedom!

Freedom can be taken away in the blink of an eye; history has shown this time and time again.

I will end with this: "What would you do without Freedom!"

The JH Complex

Thus is where the people who created the problem are unable to get past their dream of doing something great. Blinded by achievement, it's hard for them to stop the madness.

This complex has been around for decades and takes different forms. This will be good for mankind, and sometimes it works out, but when it goes wrong, the damage can be deadly.

Where did the virus come from? This is the question that keeps getting asked but what worries me is that these people are hinting around that another virus could be coming.

Bam

The variants are here, which seemed to happen very fast.

I am no science guy, but Mother Nature does not work that fast unless she has help.

Will we ever know where this virus came from? who knows? Can we learn from our mistakes? Probably not! The JHC is like tunnel vision; you only see what you want to see. There is an old saying:

"The road to hell is paved with good intentions!" Did the people in charge learn anything?

Yes, that fear is a powerful thing.

When this whole thing started, people with no emergency experience were calling the shots. Smart people, but with one mindset.

When dealing with an emergency, you have to be flexible, open-minded, take nothing off the table, and have some common sense.

Speaking of the JH complex on July 7, 2021, Dr. F was on some network telling people to just get over it and go get their vaccine shot. It's free; there are plenty of shots; what's the problem? Let go of your political beliefs and hang-ups; just go get the shot.

The vaccine can save your life and the lives of others.

In other words, get over your fears and concerns; just do as I say.

The next JH complex guy was XB, who said the government does have a right to get into your medical business.

No privacy for you, and you must take the shot!

XB has no health experience and was the AG of California, so he is a typical politician.

It's July 12, 2021, and Dr. Get Over It; **his new name** is getting upset at people who have not taken the vaccine yet. Dr. Get Over It, was flip-flopping through this whole pandemic and is a scientist who, as far as I know, has not treated one COVID-19 patient.

There were so many people in charge who were just reading reports. It's an unknown virus; ask questions, form ideas, listen to others, and be open-minded.

We only have two choices: get the vaccine or die. That's all the experts have come up with, and it's July 12, 2021.

To this day, I have not heard much about how some people survived the early days of the virus. The media failed in so many ways.

A deadly virus cripples the world, and the media goes into resistance mode. The JH complex strikes again, and lives are lost.

It's been floating around that big pharma had a role in stopping talk about therapeutics that could help people in the early stages of the virus. We will never know this answer because the media did not care to ask the question.

Next question: did the emergency use authorization stop therapeutics from being used? Did red tape cost lives? Someone explained it like this. There can be no emergency use vaccine if there is another drug that can be used.

This virus destroyed the world, and if barriers like this stood in the way, we are in a lot of trouble.

It's September 25, 2021, and the JH complex is in full force. In the month of September, we had President Biden come out again against the unvaccinated and the CDC director, Dr. RW, go against the FDA recommendation. The FDA recommends booster shots for sixty-five or older people and those at risk, not the entire general population. Dr. RW ignored the FDA, which is in charge of making sure that the drugs we take are cleared for use.

That is the function of the FDA, which gives the green light to the CDC, but Dr. RW said no thanks. I know better, and we will dish out the booster shots.

Its September 27, 2021, and to put people in a booster mood, President Biden takes a booster shot. Which is good for him because he took his two shots months ago plus he is over sixty-five.

It's October 17, 2021, and Dr. Get Over It is out again. This time, people attack him because he is telling the truth about the virus, and we can't handle the truth.

My rebuttal is that the doctor had no clue about how to deal with the unknown, and he was making it up as the virus spread. Following China's lead on lockdowns and restrictions but never looking at the big picture and the harm that it would do. The doctor never treated anybody who had COVID-19, as far as I have heard or seen.

Am I right or wrong? Someone out there must know. The JHC continues all around the world with quarantine camps, lockdowns, and arrests!

On December 21, 2021, NW reported that Dr. F and Dr. FC were intimidating other scientists who had questions about COVID-19. Other ideas and inputs were not allowed into the mix, which could have saved lives.

Why is the question?

The JHC is in all the controlled states and is causing pain from New York City to Chicago. It's a never-ending mess with restrictions and mandates. A leader must be able to look at the big picture and size it up in an emergency without making it worse. When you suffer from JHC, you are blind. You can't see the destruction you have caused and pat yourself on the back, thinking you did a great job while the forest burns around you.

The Delta Variant

It's July 21, 2021, and the Delta variant is causing cases to rise. Mask mandates in Los Angeles and Nevada are now back, with other places joining soon. The local news reported that people are now going to be sent door-to-door gathering information and educating people on the vaccines.

It has also been reported that younger people are getting infected more and going to the hospital. It's being called the pandemic of the unvaccinated by the media, politicians, doctors, and President B.

The Delta variant is more contagious, and people are being warned not to let their guard down.

All three vaccines are still in emergency use status and are still being given out to people if they choose to take a shot.

Soon the vaccines will clear the FDA, and you will be forced to take the shot. It has already started in schools, travel, and work. You have to show proof, or you will not be allowed to live your life.

It's July 26, 2021, and the king of California has announced that all state employees will need to take the vaccine. President B is mandating that federal employees get vaccinated or get tested often.

The CDC is updating its mask protocol because of the rise in cases, but it is also looking into mandates for living your life in this new normal, as they like to call it.

It's August 6, 2021, and the mayor of NYC is going to enact the vaccine passport mandate to live your life in the big apple. Other states will follow soon, and I am sure of that.

Thank God this guy never became president of America!

As the Delta variant continues to rage, President B is allowing people to flow across the southern border by the thousands. A lot of these people are testing positive for COVID-19, but it does not seem to matter, they are being transported all over the country on the tax-payer's dime. The border patrol is stretched thin and not able to do its job properly, so many people have just entered America without being tested. Border patrol; calls these people got aways, and they will be in a town near you.

47

I thought the president of the United States was supposed to protect this country and defend the Constitution.

Guess I was wrong?

The CDC and health departments seem to be calling the shots for the country, which seems weird because these people are not elected and have been sending out mixed messages. Along with their friends on social media and the mainstream news, it has gotten confusing.

Dr. Get Over It is still out with no hope and still has no real answers to this virus except vaccines up. The sad truth is that containing and controlling the unknown takes time. Studies are still being done, and no one knows all the answers yet. The doctor wants to stop COVID-19 dead in its tracks but can't pull it off without everybody getting vaccinated, according to him. Some people have natural immunity, a.k.a., have already recovered from COVID-19, which can be just as good or better than a vaccine. The doctor has not considered this to be a valid point. In every interview I have seen him in, he downplays or straight-out dismisses the information.

Scientists have a different mindset than medical doctors, which seems to be the problem throughout this pandemic.

Scientists deal with the information part of medicine.

Dealing with hypotheses and studies to find out how things work, and that takes time. Medical trials are done, and it can take years to get the information right in normal times.

We are not in one of those times right now.

Medical doctors deal with the treatment of patients, how to fix things that are broken, and, with information from scientists, provide treatment.

What we have right now is a person trying to be both. Which has caused confusion and distrust for many people, but most of all, it has caused fear.

You can read studies and reports, but treating people in real life is a different story. Medical doctors need the freedom to do what is best for their patients, and when that is taken away, it can be deadly.

I was channel surfing one day and saw this on "The Doctors," featuring Dr. DP talking about his COVID-19 experience and an antibody infusion he had received to get better. This is one of the only times I have seen or heard of another way to fight this virus besides getting vaccinated.

This doctor wanted people to know that this was an option if they needed treatment with the virus. It is covered by Medicare and Medi-Cal for emergency use and is available for patients if they ask for it. Best used in the early stages of the virus, mild to moderate, not later stages.

Dr. DP wanted people to have this information to prevent them from ending up in the hospital.

Information is a good thing in a crisis, and this doctor wanted you to know about his experience with COVID-19.

It is August 15, 2021, and the Delta variant continues to cause havoc in the world. Australia has gone into martial law, not allowing citizens to do much, and that includes talking to a neighbor. **Just keep your mouth shut and walk on. Bye.**

Sticking with Australian madness, a man sneezed in an elevator and is now on the most wanted list. JK, but he does have a warrant for his arrest. Some teens were arrested for hanging out outside and fined for not following martial law. You can't be outside, selfish people; the king has spoken.

On September 7, 2021, the madness in Australia continued with fines and curfews in effect. Soldiers who went to help with the evacuation overseas are not allowed back home yet. Australia is being run by medical tyranny, one reporter explained. Once, an awesome place turned into an island of despair.

I saw police in Australia choking a woman for not wearing a mask. A guy gets thrown down and cited for not wearing a mask. Then, to top it off, I see the king of Australia talking about how the results of his actions are a good thing. We are saving lives, he explains with the attitude of a tyrant. It must be nice to be a king and punish people who just want to live.

The reporters are warning America that this can happen to you!

Bringing it back home to America. Hospitals are filling up again from Delta, and the powers that be are having fundraisers in Napa, concerts in New York City, and a birthday party for former president OB. No mask, but you must wear one. The fundraiser was an eye-opener for how the people in charge think of us peasants. All the staff were masked, while all the guests were unmasked.

It was outside, but the image speaks volumes. I can do whatever I want, and you can't. I am important, and you are not. Screw your business, job, and freedom!

As the Delta variant continues to spread, hospitals are reporting some issues with oxygen supplies and are starting to get overwhelmed again.

In Florida, they are setting up Regeneron stations to help people with COVID-19. A Regeneron infusion can help in the early stages and breakthrough cases that might come up, but it is not being reported by the resistance media.

Why would anyone not report on something that can help people live, or worse, try to shut these places down.

It's September 3, 2021, and I just saw a report of a fifteen-year-old who caught COVID-19 and was on a ventilator for a week but has recovered. She was not vaccinated, and her message when she came out of her ordeal was for people to get vaccinated. Especially teens, because they have been on the low vaccination list.

She had trouble breathing and had to go to the hospital, which is never a good thing. We have known this from the beginning, once you are in the ICU, it's harder to come back from COVID-19, but it is happening.

Thank God and the first responders.

The reason I bring this up is because this poor child could have taken therapeutics or been given Regeneron before she ended up in an ICU bed.

On September 6, 2021, two brothers were treated at the ICU in Fresno after a trip to Las Vegas. One is in the ICU for six days, and the other for a month. They were not vaccinated and had to go to rehabilitation to fully recover from COVID-19. Their message to the unvaccinated is to get the shot; they cannot get the vaccine for ninety days. Why ninety days? I do not know because no one in the media is asking the question.

What happened to getting help in the early stages? Now, it's all about the vaccines.

The vaccines are good, but they are still not the quality they should be. It's been more about quantity than quality.

This is more evident because Dr. Get Over It has just started pushing for a third vaccine shot on top of your two.

What happened to the booster shot he was just talking about a month ago? Now it's three to be fully vaccinated!

Here is something to think about: "How many shots do you take against the flu?"

Second, is the vaccine a cure?

Two of the head people have quit the FDA. Why? It was reported that it could have something to do with the White House pushing things way too fast without the science, a.k.a. test, to back it up.

More cases of children being infected with COVID-19 are being reported as we come into September 9, 2021. The Delta variant seems to be the likely cause, as it is late into the pandemic, but more variants are on the horizon. Two other variants appeared during this time period too, but it seems those came and went. Alpha and Beta, I think, but they vanished quickly, and it was on to a new one.

It's November 19, 2021, and the next variant is reported in South Africa by a doctor. The Omicron variant is mild, according to this doctor, and there are only a few cases at this time that she is treating.

Little is known about this variant, but she is giving a heads-up to the world. We will see how the world reacts. President B imposes a travel ban on eight African countries that may pose a threat to America. Just to be on the safe side, but our border is still wide open!

Does this make sense? Seriously?

Dr. Get Over It has to chime in and claim himself to be the master of all science if anybody goes against his knowledge. **I represent science and how dare you doubt me, to question me is to question science!**

I had to make his statement stand out a little, but the science part I represent is all him. That's the truth!

The doctor from South Africa said the Omicron is mild, and I believe her more than whatever Dr. Get Over It says at this point. She is a doctor who takes care of people on the front lines. She let us all know what was going on with the Omicron. It was reported that she was surprised by the reaction.

My Body, Their Choice!

We have gotten to a dangerous level of fear in the world. Thanks to the experts and leaders who have no hope.

People are being forced to take a shot they may not need to take if they recovered from COVID-19, but that does not matter to Dr. Get Over It and the powers that be.

You will take the vaccine; we are done asking!

Your kids must take the vaccine, or no school for them!

You must take the vaccine or no work for you!

This will continue to grow because you will be kept in a constant state of fear and confusion.

When a doctor refuses to treat patients who have not gotten vaccinated and is praised for it, it has gotten pretty bad.

I thought doctors took some kind of oath, but I guess not this one.

We are even firing nurses who fought the battle in the beginning, caught COVID-19, recovered, and are now losing their jobs because they do not want to get vaccinated.

What happened to it is my body, my choice? It does not apply to COVID-19; you must comply!

President Biden has been coming out and pushing private companies and businesses to force employees to take the vaccine.

The FDA has cleared the Pfizer vaccine, which gives those who have recovered and those who are weary no choice but to get the jab if they want to have a life.

Even if you are not getting a shot, you can be denied a COVID-19 test at one clinic in Colorado if you have been seen on TV with a different political view. A clinic there denied CO of getting just a COVID-19 test because of her thoughts about the vaccine. CO has not been vaccinated but wanted to get tested because she has been traveling.

No test for you because of your political view.

It's September 7, 2021, and another doctor has denied in person treatment if her patients are not vaccinated. In Seattle, a person is denied a liver transplant because he is not vaccinated. This person has health complications due to his liver.

Another oath bites the dust!

We are seeing protests in NYC because the mayor has imposed mandates to get the vaccine or lose your job.

So much for my body, my choice?

It's October 7, 2021, and a hospital in Colorado has denied a patient having a liver transplant because she is not vaccinated. She has a donor, but the hospital said no. This is not the only hospital in Colorado that is denying care to the unvaccinated.

Denying care in the land of the free is something I never thought I would see in America.

On October 11, 2021, an anesthesiologist in LA was fired for not taking the vaccine. He is escorted out of the hospital by security.

He is like so many others who do not want to be forced to take a vaccine. It's about freedom of choice, he explains.

Another essential worker let go, like so many before him.

On October 25, 2021, there was another protest in NYC against the vaccine mandates being forced on first responders and many others who do not want the vaccine. Some of the protesters have taken the vaccine, some have recovered from COVID-19, others for religious reasons, some can't take the shot for medical reasons, and others just do not want the shot.

A lot of these people were heroes when the novel Coronavirus started, still doing their jobs when everybody else was in lockdown or getting paid to stay home.

This is how we repay our heroes after they have been in the fight the entire time.

This next story is a personal one I wanted to share.

It comes from a friend and his wife, who were not vaccinated and caught the virus. He went to the doctor to get some help but was told there were no therapeutics and told to go home.

Then he brought up Regeneron, a.k.a. antibodies, and she told him that they were not offered as treatment. This doctor did not know that my friend had checked the hospital website and that there was treatment available.

He went home and made a formal complaint, and within four hours, both of them were being treated with Regeneron.

Either this doctor knew and refused treatment on purpose because they were not vaccinated, or she is incompetent. Either way, this doctor should not be anywhere near a hospital or taking care of anybody. Common sense tells me she knew about the treatment, but since they were not vaccinated, she took it upon herself to make them suffer.

Because four hours later, she was the one calling them back for Regeneron treatments.

My friend made his choice and learned a lesson, but unfortunately, the doctor who sent them home probably has not. My fear is that she will do this to another person who will not be as lucky. She will send them home only to have them end up in an ICU bed later because she refused treatment.

Those unvaccinated people need to pay for not getting the vaccine, which seems to be the attitude of so many people, including this doctor.

Oath breaker or death dealer?

On the other side of the coin, a friend took the route of vitamin D and C, zinc, and a multivitamin for the whole two years, plus masked up where needed. He went on a diet and exercised more, which is always a good thing. He is a diabetic, but he was never scared of the virus because he tried to make his immune system stronger.

My friend even took a test to see if he had caught COVID-19 and had antibodies, but he didn't, so he continued to keep up with what he was doing.

The day finally came when he took his first shot. It was hard to take something he felt he did not need because he felt fine. He had just been out living life and was around people all the time. After he took the shot, he cried and wished he would have died instead.

I am sure that with all the haters out there—some people would say he should have died, but those people live in fear and hate.

JR, JK, the D and G network, social media, and the rest of the doom squad.

I asked him why he cried, and he said, "I lost something today!"

I will let the reader figure out what he lost!

Everybody has a different body and condition; one size does not fit all when it comes to health issues. That's just a fact.

Treatments vary from person to person!

It's October 30, 2021, and the FDA has approved the Pfizer vaccine for emergency use on five- to eleven-year-old children.

A child of God, but their choice, I guess?

A surgeon was fired for standing up for parents at a school board meeting because of mask mandates. The line that stuck out to me was, "Is that God gave these children to the parents, not to you."

Do we really need schoolboards?

It's November 5, 2021, and the CDC has approved the vaccine for children ages five to eleven. The FDA has cleared it, but one of the board members says this. "We have to wait and see how it affects the children in this age group, he says out loud."

So let's get this straight: a small study is done on five- and eleven-year-old kids cleared by the FDA. The side effects on these children are not totally known yet, but these people want you to give it to your children.

Does that sound like science, as your children are being used as guinea pigs?

The king of California has survived his recall, and now it's time for children to get a vaccine if they want to live their lives too.

Some parents are ready, and some are not, but the doom and gloom channel has you covered with little kids getting the shot. They are even bringing out Big Bird and his gang to give it that extra touch.

The doom and gloom network was anti-vaccine before because of the bad orange man, but now it's get the shot, little children.

On December 28, 2021, a Boston police officer is going to be fired because she is not vaccinated. She is pregnant, so she does not want the vaccine, but the mayor of Boston is sticking to her mandate. The officer asked the mayor if she would sign an agreement taking responsibility if she were to take the vaccine and something bad happened to her or her unborn child.

No response from the mayor, of course.

There really is no study set in stone about the effects of the vaccines on pregnant women after two years. As a matter of fact, we seem to be getting a lot of information from other countries and only a little from the US medical field. Things are still all over the map!

The WHO has chimed in on children a little bit because of the Omicron variant, but I have not seen much of them lately, but they did make a statement on keeping children in masks. It's not a good thing for children to be masked up all the time!

A little late in the game for the WHO! We have hit the two-year mark!

Some people have already been fighting for no mask, and others arc too fearful to let go of the mask. We will find out the damage done to the children in the years to come, but for now, the fight continues.

Misinformation and Follow the Science?

WE HAVE BEEN HEARING this throughout the whole pandemic. Follow the science and misinformation?

We used to have this thing called free speech and free expression of thought, but no more in the land of the free.

During our greatest time of need, people with other ideas and thoughts were silenced. Doctors who were treating patients with the Coronavirus in the early days were shut down by FB and TW. Misinformation they touted, but what if these treatments saved lives?

It did not matter to FB or TW billionaires.

Some politicians banned therapeutics that were being used to help people. Some doctors who continued to treat people in this way lost their jobs and, in some cases, lost their license to practice medicine.

It did not matter to these politicians. These doctors are wrong, and we are right to do this. No more treatments for you, only an ICU bed and death.

Today is August 10, 2021, and the never-ending chart on the side of the screen with cases and deaths continues on one network. **Doom and gloom 24/7**

The network even had a child come out and talk about the importance of wearing a mask. I know that a child can get COVID-19, but to use a child in this way this far into the pandemic is pretty disturbing. Children are pretty strong when dealing with the virus, so having this child come out seemed to be a scare tactic aimed at parents because of the Delta variant.

The CDC is still gathering data on this variant, and President Biden is pushing for the FDA to clear at least one of the vaccines.

On August 11, 2021, they had a nurse talking about the importance of getting the vaccine and her experiences with the new spike in cases.

The sad truth is that you could vaccinate the whole world and there would still be cases. We are still gathering data and learning about COVID-19. That is why it takes years to get full FDA approval, but in the case of COVID-19, I see approval sooner.

It is August 11, 2021, for reference countdown.

On August 23, 2021, the Pfizer vaccine will be the first vaccine approved by the FDA, twelve days from the reference countdown.

We have been told to "follow the science," but only one side of the story is being told to most of the public. Other doctors and scientists were being shut out of this whole process.

The question I pose to the reader is, "Why were they shut down?"

A second or third opinion from other doctors should have been welcomed. If something were wrong with you, wouldn't you want more information?

If a doctor doesn't work out, do you stay with the same one or try someone new?

We are all humans and make mistakes, but when push comes to shove, you want the best information you can receive in a crisis; instead, we got resistance and censorship.

So many people cried misinformation, but was it really all misinformation or just politics and money at play?

Some say big pharma had a role to play in the early days of the pandemic. We will never know because the media had an agenda to get President Trump out of office.

Question to the reader: "Why was it right to try so hard to get through the government?"

A. Politics
B. Money
C. Power
D. All the above

In the middle of a world emergency, anything that could have saved a life should have been used, not dismissed.

Who really costs lives in the end?

A. Politicians
B. Media
C. Social media
D. Scientists
E. All the above

There was a story about JR and ivermectin that saved his life, but it was quickly described as a horse drug by many in the media. Ivermectin can be used on horses, but also on people with a doctor who knows what he is doing. JR survived his COVID-19 ordeal, but because of the reaction from the media, he was dishing out misinformation.

How dare he live and spread lies!

You can't even have natural immunity, according to some people. We have to look into it more, says Dr. Get Over It. It's been over a year, and the DOCTOR has no clue but wants you to take a vaccine that is not up to snuff yet.

What is the CDC actually doing?

Are they studying language and putting out new words for us to use?

Misinformation YouTube cried when it canceled a podcast between a doctor and SH, which gave another look into the mandates being imposed on Americans.

You are mandating a vaccine that has an expiration date and causing distrust in the medical field, the doctor explained.

The vaccine wears off over time and is not as strong as natural immunity. This is something that has been studied but has been totally blown off by so many people. Misinformation, disinformation, lies, and conspiracy theories made them cry in anger and hatred.

Some people have no shame and should take a good look at themselves. Mirror—mirror on the wall who is the dumbest one of all, we can take our pick. The list is long and wide!

The CDC has no information on the people who recovered from the virus, as far as I have seen or heard. **You would think this would be important information to find out!**

Some studies from other countries say that natural immunity lasts longer and is stronger, but that has been dismissed by the CDC. You still need the vaccine. Two years into this hell, and this is the best we have to offer.

Follow the science from RW because that's it. Get vaccinated or die. We pay millions of dollars to this agency, and this is what we get for our money.

America needs a refund!

On November 18, 2021, Dr. SA came out and reported on the task force that was in charge when he came in to help. It was not a pretty picture that he painted of the three main people. Dr. F was one of them, so it makes sense why we are in mandate mode now.

We are guinea pigs being tested on by leaders who do not want this pandemic to end.

Whenever there was a solution made to help, the resistance had to shoot it down. The so-called experts and big pharma did not want any therapeutics to be the answer because there was no money to be made.

It's like Dr. Frankenstein protecting his creation, no matter the cost. The monster must survive!

Senator RP confirmed this in late December of 2021. The people in charge now are holding back on therapeutics that would help people. Monoclonal antibodies and other meds are being rationed or all-out denied to people.

So ask yourself this question: "If it were all about saving lives, then why would you deny or ration care?" It's a sad thing to say, but true! Everything should have been on the table, but the resistance shot any hope down.

A reminder of the congresswomen who thanked President Trump. Who silenced her? Does that sound like someone you should trust when your life is on the line?

Dr. FC of the NIH said on air on December 19, 2021, that some people just wanted this pandemic to rip. The report in question did not say that. It's called the Great Barrington report; check it out.

I want the reader to search for the answers to this one themselves.

Dr. FC also said that nothing was off the table and that he was trying to stop misinformation. If that was the case, then why go against therapeutics?

What do these agencies actually do?

On December 21, 2021, the president came out and gave a speech on how he is going to battle the Omicron variant. I did not watch this speech because it was going to be the same old thing. Let's blame the unvaccinated!

No inspiration or confidence! Not worth watching at this point.

On December 22, 2021, a Pfizer pill is authorized for emergency use, but supplies were limited. The Merck pill has not been cleared yet.

What do you know? It's December 23, 2021, and the Merck pill has been approved for emergency use! We have two pills in the toolbox; let's see if doctors will be allowed to do their job now.

Pfizer is rolling in the money on vaccines and pills now, so I guess doctors will be allowed to move forward.

It's been close to two years, and this is the first pill the FDA has cleared for emergency use. The FDA needs an overhaul because there were other treatments being used by doctors that were dismissed.

All these agencies failed in one way or another.

Case in point: it's December 27, 2021, and we are short on COVID-19 test kits for America. The people in charge have put everybody in panic mode again, so no test kits are available for mass use. Test kits are on order, but not enough at this time, so they will be rationed, it is my guess.

There was a report that the White House was told about the need for test kits in November 2021 but decided not to move on the advice. Misinformation, or is it true?

Who knows at this point!

Because on December 27, 2021, the president said there is no federal solution for the pandemic. It may be better handled at the state level. **So why the national push for mandates?**

Like no domestic flights without a vaccine passport, Dr. Get Over It is for this idea!

So no flying to Vegas for you unvaccinated people.

In the same breath, Dr. Get Over It talks about taking nothing off the table, but he still has blown off natural immunity and early treatment options. These two things never made it to his table, it seems.

Misinformation or following the science?

Instead, we get mandates and punishment for trying to survive a pandemic. The resistance strikes again!

I have seen certain doctors calling for a more targeted approach and just getting the systematic people tested instead of the whole population, but that goes against the fear that needs to keep going.

The fear of death and suffering for the unvaccinated, JK the White House dude blasted on one network just before Christmas. **What a guy? Merry doom and gloomy Christmas to you!**

When I think the experts and the people in charge can't make things worse, they always prove me wrong.

The Mandates are Coming... the Mandates are Coming

IN OUR DARKEST HOUR, the worst in people comes out. We have mandates from President B, mayors, governors, and employers, and if you do not comply, you will not be able to live your life like you used to.

The mayor of NYC has started his segregation plan for the vaccinated and unvaccinated.

I would expect nothing else from this guy; he has no shame in his game.

A person in Seattle is being denied a liver transplant because he is not vaccinated. This person has health complications due to his liver.

A Texas judge orders kids to wear masks and restaurants to do the same for all employees and customers. Thanks, Judge CJ; you are a class act.

This is what America has become under fear, and this is what the government that caused this pandemic wanted.

Democracy and freedom suck; we are the future, and our way is better.

One case in New Zealand has triggered a lockdown in the town of Auckland for seven days.

Japan is also going into lockdown as cases surge.

The people of France are back out protesting the mandates.

You had a leader in Australia actually saying you couldn't drink a beer outside without your mask on. Drink through your mask, I guess? How stupid the world has become under COVID-19!

Mandates, threats, and arrests have become the norm in the world.

A woman had her child taken from her because she was not vaccinated. A judge laid down this verdict until she got vaccinated, which she did because she missed her child.

What a piece of crap, judge! No wonder there is no trust in the justice system anymore.

Remember, this is not the only judge who wanted to play God during the pandemic.

Today is the day I knew was coming. It's September 9, 2021, and President B has just called for a nationwide mandate on vaccines. It is the pandemic of the unvaccinated, and his patience has worn thin. A few months ago, he said he would not do mandates, but of course, he lied; career politicians always do.

He explained that it's not about freedom or personal choice but about saving lives. If it were truly about saving lives, there would have been less opposition to doctors who were treating patients in the beginning. All we have had is resistance, and now we have the force of the federal government.

It sounds like a dictator to me, not a president of America.

Dr. Get Over It is all on board, along with the usual suspects. The doctor was even on Comedy Central with TN, and he was happy about mandates. It has been reported that the doctor knew and cleared the funds that started the pandemic out of China. The only doctor that we have been listening to through this whole thing is this guy, and he was on Comedy Central, which fits because he has become a joke.

This virus is still a mystery in many ways. No one has all the answers, but forcing people to get a vaccine that is still not the quality it should be is mind-blowing. Some Republican governors are going to fight back, and we will see what the courts do.

I have little faith in our judges these days but even less faith in most of our leaders.

It is September 19, 2021, and the president has limited the supply of Regeneron to Florida in the name of equity, according to JS. Florida gets 30 percent of what it was receiving, which proves that it's all about power. This new administration is going after a governor who is trying to save lives and protect our freedom at the same time.

Politicians all over the world lockdown and punish people if they do not comply with their mandates, even in the land of the free.

Lucky for us, we have the Constitution and people who still believe in liberty and freedom in this country.

Because without the protection of our founding documents, we would be in more trouble. For now, it's keeping the vultures at bay. In parts of America, they do not care about the Constitution or freedom; it's do as I say or else!

Some people believe in freedom, and some believe in chaos. I saw this story in November of 2021. Australia has set up quarantine camps for people. What is their crime? Having COVID-19 or not being vaccinated? Take your pick because it does not matter in the land down below.

Three people escaped from the camp, and a manhunt began. A woman is offered drugs because she is having difficulty being locked up. A guy in an elevator did not have a mask on, and there was a warrant for his arrest. A city leader is locked up because he spoke up about the mandates. Someone told me that Australia used to be a penal colony, and it looks like it is again if you don't follow the rules!

Bringing it back to NYC, comrade D is calling for a full city mandate on the private sector and kids on his way out the door. Merry Christmas, and take your shot!

Some people do not know when they are in a world of hurt. NYC was hit hard in the beginning and is still getting hit by the people in charge. The people of NYC elected a new mayor; we will see how he does.

It's been some time since we have heard anything out of China, but the word is that they are locking people in their homes again. China is hosting the Winter Olympics but is locking up people with COVID-19, so why are countries sending their athletes there?

You are going to a country where you are bound by their rules and where all this started. The advice from the people in charge is to take a burner phone. America's NP warns the athletes not to make any political statements and to just compete. I wish all who travel there good luck!

In Canada, the PM has pushed a lot of citizens too far with his mandates, and there is going to be a mass protest. This would not be the last protest in Canada, and the next one was going to start a movement that would have the world watching. **The Freedom Convoy is about to begin!**

Changes but Still the Same

WE WILL START WITH the new governor of New York City, who took the AC spot after he resigned. AC still thinks he did nothing wrong when he gave the final speech.

The new governor, KH, continues the same plan as the old, but with this added. COVID-19 vaccines come "from God to us," and appealed to the people to spread the word to the vaccine holdouts, who she said are ignoring God. This speech was at the CC Center in Brooklyn on September 16, 2021.

NYC is also firing people who have not gotten the vaccine and calling for outside help from other countries and states. The weird thing is that NYC is one of the most vaccinated states in the country but has some of the worst restrictions.

Next up!

The king of California has survived his recall and is ready to take it out on Californians. He has mandated that all kids who are eligible for the vaccine must get it in order to go to school.

What else is going on?

There is a new pill that can help in the fight against COVID-19, but it still needs approval from the FDA. I just saw this on October 1, 2021, but like anything that can help, it is quickly questioned by the doom and gloom channel.

President Biden continues his attack on the unvaccinated, with OSHA getting involved with a new safety protocol. President B is also talking about fining companies that do not have all their employees vaccinated for $75,000 to $750,000, even if it's only one employee you will pay. Smaller companies and businesses will be fined too, at a smaller amount of five to fourteen thousand.

People have been suffering for over a year, and the pain continues, but not all of it is coming from the virus.

Dr. Get Over It is at it again, talking about holiday restrictions. It's only October 4, 2021, and he is already talking about the rules that we all know by now.

Life has moved on for many people because we need to live and make a living. Dr. Get Over It does not seem to understand that he is running behind a lot of the data, and trust in him has fallen.

It's also been reported that Dr. FC from the NIH will be leaving the agency soon. We have heard from this doctor a few times during the pandemic, but he is not the one calling the shots. It's all about Dr. F and his own documentary, **coming to you soon.**

It's January 2, 2022, and NYC has a new mayor with the same plan; the mandates will stay in place.

I put this entry here because NYC wanted to change but got the same in EA. Good luck to the people of NYC.

The NYC police are even throwing people out of Burger King for not being vaccinated or masked up. No whopper for you, little kid; that goes for your mother too!

There is a change in some leaders, but it's not about science; it's about politics. They see that people are getting tired and have had enough of the mandates. It's getting harder to keep the fear going, but they are trying. **The doom and gloom network never lets up on the fear!**

KH, the temporary governor of NYC, is lifting the mask mandates on businesses but keeping them in the schools. The kids still need to wear a mask in class.

Two years, going on three, and these poor kids still need to have a mask on. Kids can adapt to this easier than adults. Let's train the kids to have a mask on their faces forever, which seems to be the mentality of so many people.

Children are not pets to be trained or kept masked up! Most kids can handle COVID-19, according to the data. We are moving into year three, and for some leaders, nothing has changed except their masks can come off, but not your kids.

I feel sorry for the children who depended on the adults to have some kind of common sense but failed them in the end. Kids are fearless; it's the adults that are scared.

What kind of world are the children of the pandemic going to live in? Only time will tell!

Free States Versus Controlled States

DURING THIS PANDEMIC, YOU could see the difference in leadership. Where freedom and common sense were used to not cripple people just trying to survive, and where fear was used to control people just trying to survive.

The government became worse than the virus.

The government put friend against friend and neighbor against neighbor. Eighteen months of pain, and the people in charge are loving their power.

In the controlled states, you **must take the vaccine** or lose your job; you can't go to a restaurant or concert, and your children can't go to school. You need a vaccine passport to live your life, we have spoken. Sounds like the old South to me. Do as I say, or else!

The free states are trying to balance our rights and our health. Here is all the information, and you can decide when you will get your treatment. You can get the vaccine, Regeneron, or, if you have already recovered from COVID-19, wait for treatment if needed. Natural immunity has been embraced by the free states but totally disregarded by the CDC, FDA, Dr. F, and the controlled states.

This far into this pandemic, it makes you wonder what the CDC is doing.

The WHO has been pretty quiet, but Dr. Get Over It is out making his TV rounds.

Many people are moving to free states like Florida and Texas because the controlled state leaders are destroying people's lives with mandates. The South has always hated freedom, and the pandemic has shown us that not much has changed from the past. It has always been about control and division with the South.

There was an old saying, if you know your history, "The south shall rise again!" Tyranny has no limits for those who crave power more than liberty.

Fear is the name of the game! Keeping you scared gives them control.

Here is an example: The new governor of NYC has just signed an executive order to cancel elective procedures.

No emergency—no surgery for you! The damage this can do is scary, but there is a new variant, so this governor feels like this is a good idea. We will see what happens.

Sticking with the new governor has reimposed indoor mask mandates, so the King of California had to do it too! How nice of them!

Merry Christmas 2021 from the king and queen!

The court jester of NYC is on his way out, but the damage he has done is amazing. DB thinks businesses should be the vaccine police, and he is not alone in his madness. There has been so much pain and suffering from the pandemic. Lives lost, businesses gone forever, depression, suicide, addiction, and more. So what do the vultures do? Make you choose between providing for your family or getting a vaccine you may not need.

Meanwhile, in the free states of America, they are enjoying their Christmas with their families and friends! Mask-free if they like; it's up to them, not the government. Florida is leading the charge for freedom. The governor said he would not allow people to lose their jobs over vaccine status. People still have a right to choose what they put into their bodies, and he is not allowing businesses in his state to place mandates on their employees.

The president of the free world does not agree with the free state governors of America.

It's almost a new year, and the Omicron variant continues to spread, but the haters still have to hate and have a double standard.

Let's start with NP buying a vacation home in the great free state of Florida. It must be nice to be that arrogant and rich.

Next is the congresswoman from NYC, a.k.a. Verruca Salt, having fun in the free state of Florida while the people of NYC have to deal with COVID-19 restrictions. She has hated the governor of Florida for months, and now she is there celebrating the new year in the state she railed against. **No shame in her game, obviously.**

We can't forget celebs coming down to Florida for the MC party. Everybody here is vaccinated, and the masked MC screamed at the crowd. Question: then why did you come to Florida MC when you could have stayed in your regulated town?

All these people want freedom for themselves but will deny it for you. They all live in controlled states but will not do anything to change course.

Let's go to a free state instead and party because we can't do it where we live.

Some people who live in free states are worried because they are seeing more people coming from controlled states moving into their areas. This is a free country, and you can move to any state you want to, but please do not ruin my state like the one you left. Their concern is valid because if these people vote the same way, the free states will be gone, and there will be nowhere to run.

California and NYC have some of the biggest movers to free states. What's the common denominator among all the controlled states?

You should know the answer because you voted them in!

Like Congressman ES of California, who went down to the free state of Florida too. It must be nice to have a taste of freedom instead of lockdowns and restrictions.

The governor of Florida says he has heard of other politicians coming down for a taste of freedom, but he is gracious; he has not said who these people are. That will be up to the freedom-loving people of Florida to point out the haters.

We have had so many leaders flaunt their double standards in the face of freedom-loving people, and yet, for some strange reason, these same people still remain in power.

The list is a mile long, so I guess people like being used and abused by lying politicians. That's all I can come up with, because I see no logic in electing the same people who have failed you time and time again.

Only this time, we are dealing with a pandemic.

America is a free country for now, but that can all change in the blink of an eye at this point. The free states are leading the way, and the controlled states will follow in the end because they have to, not because they want to. The pandemic will eventually slow down, but the power-hungry will never stop.

Freedom is a bad word for many people today. It means something different to different people, but this is the definition of **freedom**: the power or right to act, speak, or think without hindrance. Or if that does not work for you, try this one: absence of subjection to foreign domination or despotic government.

So I ask the reader this important question. Did the people making the rules think about your freedom when they were closing everything down?

The End of 2021

L OOKING BACK THROUGH THIS nightmare, I pose this question to the reader. "Did the people in charge really do all they could to save lives?"

Did they make smart decisions?

Did the media and social media cost lives in their reporting?

A health emergency requires clear thinking and honest answers, not political agendas. Someone asked me if there was an end to this pandemic, and I said no.

The people in power want this to continue!

A virus destroyed the world, and how did the world respond?

No one knew anything but seemed to take China's approach, and it continues to this day in many countries.

The sad truth is that the world was blindsided. You can only mitigate it at this point. The time for containment passed over two years ago. Trying to control a new virus is hard.

Unfortunately, most of the so-called leaders around the world have lost their minds.

It's become more about power than saving lives at this point.

I gave them the benefit of the doubt in the beginning, but that all changed when fifteen days turned into two years.

We were told about flattening the curve and not overwhelming the hospitals. Now it's about the cases and mandates.

The definition of mitigate is to make it less severe, serious, or painful.

I ask the reader this question: Are your leaders mitigating?

You cannot live your life unless you get a vaccine and a passport to match.

Does that sound like mitigation?

The people in charge have become worse than the pandemic. They have used fear, anger, and hate to go after people and take away their right to live unless they comply.

When I think back about how all this began and the actions taken, I am truly saddened. I try to see the world as it is, not as I wish it to be.

If we are being truly honest, "No one was going to stop this virus once it started." Second, hatred blinded many in this country to any solution. I have given you examples of silencing people, and that costs lives.

Imagine the lives that could have been saved if there had been no resistance.

We had no vaccines then, but doctors were treating patients with what they had in their toolbox, but that was not allowed. **Lives were lost thanks to the resistance.**

In the beginning, we knew very little about the novel Coronavirus, but two years later, we had three vaccines. Which is good news, but the world is being run by leaders who were still living in March of 2020 when this nightmare began.

We had two different approaches to a pandemic; which leader made things worse?

When you have an emergency, you take nothing off the table that can save a life. Did that happen?

It should have been all hands on deck, but did that happen?

This is how I will break it down in the end! No BS

President Trump and his team were in the heart of the storm with no vaccine, not enough supplies, and battling the unknown. The experts recommended lockdowns, and he did it while the team was trying to figure out a game plan.

President Trump tried to give solutions to the novel Coronavirus in the beginning, but the resistance was not having it. Lives lost!

There was communication between the state leaders. It did not matter what state they were in; they got what they needed. It took time because the supplies were low, but help did come. Regardless of the crap talk and insults, the president did his job for the states and the country.

President Trump wanted schools to open and people to get back to work because he saw the toll it took on so many people, but the resistance was not having that either.

There is no way a vaccine can be made in record time. He was mocked and dismissed until it became a reality. Let's jump in line and get the vaccine now that the bad orange man is gone.

The free states were the first to start the process of fully opening, and they were blasted by the media and politicians who were still in lockdown mode.

Many in this country wanted a national lockdown and a national plan, but the president left it up to the states, per the Constitution. He did not go mandate crazy on the nation or regulate this country to death. The feds were the incident command center, the governor and mayors were operations and logistics, and Congress was finance. It was a work in progress, but it was working.

When President forty-five left office, we had three vaccines in emergency use, and things were starting to open up, but that would all change in 2021.

In 2021, President Biden took the helm, and it started off with executive orders. The push for more mandates would soon follow. Mask mandates for his first one hundred days were first, and then came the vaccine mandates. Which was the final straw for some in this country!

Millions of people had already started getting the vaccine on their own, but that was not good enough. We need more people vaccinated, so let's pawn it off on businesses to do more and use OSHA to get around the Constitution.

Suppose a year of lockdowns and all the hell that came with it was not enough. Let's force people to get a vaccine! This is what happened next: People started quitting their jobs, some were just fired, some protested, some moved to a free state, and the list goes on.

The courts got involved and stopped some of the mandates at different levels of the spectrum, but this administration kept doubling down and still pushed businesses to make mandates, a.k.a. requirements.

No matter what the court says, we say do it anyway!

Many big companies and businesses did what the president asked, a.k.a. ordered. Let's be honest!

The smaller businesses were already hurting because of staffing. A lot of people were still getting paid to stay home, and the vaccine mandates were just making things worse. Big businesses can afford all the rules and regulations, but small businesses can't!

Mandates were being pushed by our so-called experts and people in charge who do not live in the world most of us live in. It's always easy to be the one making the rules and having no consequences for the damage it may cause to someone else.

Quick question. This administration was given three vaccines, so why are things worse? Why all the mandates and rules for a virus that you will never control?

Speaking of control, a court just put back in place the nationwide vaccine mandate. On to the Supreme Court, we go! We will see what they do.

To have complete strangers decide the fate of America is uneasy. We may lose our freedom to decide what we put in our bodies, and once that is gone, it will be gone forever. The people who did this will never stop pushing for more power and control. The country that caused this would have won. America is done! The sad thing is, we did it to ourselves.

In the end, hate and fear destroy the world, but there are still people willing to fight for freedom and liberty. People who believe in hope and faith!

Today is Christmas Day, December 25, 2021. Today's entry is about prayer, hope, and love! A prayer for all those who lost loved ones, hope for all who remain, and love for a world in pain.

After Action Review

Looking back two years, "What could have been done better?"

1. Being more open-minded about treatments that could have helped people.
2. Not having tunnel vision, a.k.a. JHC
3. Working as a team instead of an opponent
4. Keeping politics out of a health emergency
5. Better communication
6. Be honest with yourself and the American people.
7. Get off social media, (FB, TW).
8. No mandates or vaccine passports
9. Talk to your own doctor.
10. Stop watching the doom and gloom channels

A New Year 2022

I WAS GOING TO STOP writing this journal in 2022 but changed my mind because no one was going to tell the story of the people. Some people can give up their freedom easily, but some people know the end game.

Control, transformation, agenda, that's it.

We know that the vaccines do not stop the transmission of the virus. The vaccinated, unvaccinated and even the people who were naturally infected, Omicron can hit anyone, but president b is still blasting the unvaccinated.

Some doctors state that the Omicron variant is COVID-19 changing into a weaker variant because it does not get deep into the lungs, like original COVID-19 or it's other variants. It may be more contagious but does not have the same kick, but they are still studying cases.

You even had Dr. RM, the scientist who helped create the mRNA for the vaccines come out and talk about Omicron. He also commented on some of the publics concerns about the vaccine side effects. A debate that was shut down by social media and never shown on mainstream media.

Misinformation they cry!

In 2022 we also have the CDC going around the protocol that gives the green light for medicines. Their science experts are ignored by the bosses to get boosters out to your kids. Let's skip a step and see what happens?

The CDC is even changing the quarantine time from 10 days to 5 days, because of work shortages. RW comes out to explain the new guidelines, but does it actually follow the science?

You can decide if you check their website.

It's January 7, 2022, and the Supreme court is hearing cases on the mandates, president B is trying to impose on the American people. We already know where three judges stand even before the case is presented.

One judge says that the Omicron variant is more deadly than Delta. False. Then goes on to say that one hundred thousand children are in serious condition and on ventilators. **False**. It's not a vaccine mandate. False.

These people sit on the highest court in the land and will decide your fate based on misinformation. It comes down to their ideology in the end, not the Constitution.

It's also on January 7, 2022, that I see the president give remarks on how the virus is here to stay in some form.

So the president of the free world wants you to stick a vaccine in your body that is not a cure. If you do not comply, you will lose the right to live freely in this country.

President B is not going to shut down the virus, but he will shut you down. You will lose your individual freedom over your body and your life. **Welcome to Biden's America.**

The Supreme Court verdict is out today, January 13, 2022. The mandate on large businesses and Osha crap is shot down. The mandate for some healthcare workers is upheld. This is what most people predicted!

But this fight for freedom is not over because the virus is not over. The people in charge will not give up their power easily. You will suffer in the controlled states with mandates and threats.

It's January 18, 2022, and I see this story on TCT. A reporter has footage from different countries around the world. People who are seeing their freedom taken away by those in charge, must be vaccinated or punished. People from Italy, France, and countries I have never heard of are crying out for freedom.

Are the leaders listening? In many countries, the answer is no. Here in America, we are hanging on by a thread.

We have a president who does not believe in freedom!

He said it himself. "Freedom, come on."

It's January 19, 2022, and the PM of the UK has finally said no more mandate madness! He is the first world leader to do this. We will see if any other leader follows his lead.

It's January 25, 2022, and the FDA is pulling monoclonal antibodies from Florida because they say they're not working on the Omicron variant. Florida must close shop in its centers! The FDA gave this type of treatment an emergency use authorization, but now the emergency is over, I guess?

This agency needs an overhaul because pulling a life-saving treatment does not sound like a smart idea.

Are we still dealing with a pandemic or not, FDA?

Now Pfizer wants the FDA to clear vaccines for four- to eleven-year-old kids and even infants. We will see what the FDA does.

The mandate madness is starting to fade in the controlled states because of the poll numbers, not because of science. Let's be honest about this, because if these people could keep you in lockdown forever, they would.

We have had controlled state leaders breaking their own rules from the beginning of this pandemic. Imposing rules on you while they break the rules. I held my breath for a photo. The mayor of Los Angeles held his breath in the photo, so that was his excuse. SA didn't wear a mask, but all the children around her did. That picture says it all! Do as I say, not as I do!

We have had kids threatened with trespassing and suspension if they do not wear a mask in some school districts. Some leaders are even threatening child protective services for the parents.

All these so-called leaders have no business being public officials, especially when it comes to your kids!

Some students are starting to stand up to the dictators of the school by walking out, but these boards do not care because they are protected by a union.

This next entry is a month off because of COVID-19 burn-out! No February

It's March 1, 2022, and the president is about to give the state of the union address. The message is: "If you are vaccinated, no more masks." The chamber is filled, and most of the people are not masked, which is a good thing. "The CDC has given its blessing for the vaccinated," the president announces. No blaming the unvaccinated this time.

"It's your choice" seems to be the new answer for the time being. We have been here before, déjà vu!

The president is masked up at an event later, which is cool, but the media is required to wear them, so nothing has changed for him. Politicians have elections coming up in November, so a lot of these mandate tyrants are changing course, betting that all the pain and suffering they caused will be forgotten by you.

Most likely it will be; look no further than the king of California surviving his recall. California and NYC love getting screwed, it seems.

The American version of the freedom convoy is slowing coming into Washington, DC, and they are going to talk to lawmakers. Some of the mandates are slowly being lifted in controlled states, but the issue has not gone away completely.

Kids are still having to wear masks in some schools, and vaccines are still being forced on people in some states, but a war has broken out in Ukraine, and the news has shifted.

You catch a little COVID-19 news on the local stations and on the doom-gloom network. The last report was still about cases and mandates that I saw on the networks.

Right now, it's about the war in Ukraine, so I will stop writing for a bit. It's March 9, 2022.

I did catch this about the convoy on March 15, 2022. It has been blocked from getting too close to the capital. The trucks are there but are being held back by law enforcement. The mayor and leaders in Washington, DC, seem to be on the ball this time, but you're out of luck when it comes to your safety. Today is also the official day of the COVID-19 nightmare, according to TC. Two years in, and the CEO of Pfizer is talking about a fourth shot because three is not enough.

The only time you should need four shots is in a bar! Jack Daniels or Jose, the choice is yours!

It should be obvious to anyone that the vaccines are not up to par and should not be forced on anyone at this point in the pandemic. The people in charge know this deep down but do not care, in my opinion. They have to keep the fear and confusion going, or they can't keep the power they crave.

Point in case!

The news of another variant is on the move, according to Dr. Get Over It, and the CDC needs more money to do studies. We will be on variant fifty before people realize the damage that has been done by so many of the experts.

It's March 16, 2022, and China seems to be having another outbreak and locking people down again. Europe is also having some outbreaks, but we are only getting a little information because of the war overseas.

The fight over the pandemic is not over, and we are going into its third year. I am seeing commercials about long-time COVID now, which shows me that the people in charge are not giving up the fear campaign.

It is kind of hard to trust people who do not have all the answers yet. This is still a new virus, and it keeps changing according to them, but has it really changed that much?

We still have the same guidelines in some states and countries. So when will this pandemic end? No one knows!

On April 1, 2022, I see an old 2004 news interview with Dr. F talking about natural immunity when it deals with the flu. Natural immunity is more potent than a vaccine for the flu. So he does know about natural immunity but has held back on COVID-19 natural immunity. The question is, why?

Every time there was a sign of hope or something that could help, Dr. F pretty much shot it down. To this day, we still have no real studies on those who have recovered from COVID.

Granted, it's a new virus, but there has to be a basic foundation and an open mind to the unknown.

Dr. Get Over It was asked if the lockdowns helped and his answer was yes, lockdowns did save lives.

I actually agreed with Dr. F in the beginning, like most people did, but over time that all changed. Something did not seem right, and I lost trust in our government to do the right thing! How about you?

Speaking of not trusting the government, the Democratic Party in California is making bills to keep some COVID-19 rules in place forever. Punishment for misinformation, vaccine mandates for all employees, and the list goes on. Do you still think it's about the virus and saving lives three years in?

The new mayor of NYC: "EA is allowing performers and sportspeople to get a free pass, but for the rest of NY, you must obey. Mandates remain for you and your toddlers too." The people of NY got what they wanted, I guess?

President B is canceling title forty-two at the border on May 23, 2022, so I guess the pandemic is over! No more mandates for anyone!

Wishful thinking, but no chance for you. You are an American citizen, and you mean nothing to the vultures in government!

The federal mandates will stay in place, but you can come across the border freely.

It's all about power and money—your money and their power!

A few Democratic members of Congress have tested positive for the virus after a conference, but we have no solid proof that they're positive as NP gets close to President B at a party. NP says she is asymptomatic, which is a real thing, and she has been vaccinated. Point taken and good news, but we are just supposed to take their word for it when NP and her funky bunch are trying to pass another bill dealing with COVID relief.

All these people have lied in the past, but their lies affect a whole country. I wish them well, but I do not believe them. It is a sad thing to say, but they have proven time and time again that they cannot be trusted.

There is an old saying: "Fool me once, shame on you. Fool me twice, shame on me!"

Catching this story on April 8, 2022, the FDA has okayed booster shot number four and has dismissed their own experts in the agency.

Is it a good thing to put a fourth shot into your body?

What are the side effects of a fourth shot?

Questions with no real answers yet!

It has also been reported that the federal government has bought up monoclonal antibodies, so they control the life-saving treatment instead of the private sector.

Let's control life-saving treatments. Still think they care?

Dr. Get Over It has finally come to the fact that COVID is going to be a part of life for some time. That is the sad reality of this pandemic. Another sad thing is that the doctor and the vultures are always ready to strike again.

Look no further than overseas.

China has locked down Shanghai, and it is a hard thing to watch as people are forced to give up their freedom. One of the stories is of the city at night and the screams of its citizens from all the buildings. Another is of a child being loaded into a van, and one man is screaming for food.

Heartbreaking images!

There is a new variant called BA.2 that has been reported, but it is not getting much news coverage. So I am shocked but not surprised by China's actions. The local news and mainstream news have been pretty quiet about this variant. The doom and gloom network has even been pretty quiet, but it never lets you forget that COVID is still around. **Fear is always the name of the game!**

On the misinformation front, the jester of Canada, JT, is calling for the censorship of journalists, he does not agree with. JT is pushing for a license to censor free speech about COVID-19. Let's follow the science and squash all dissent. I the jester command you!

It's April 19, 2022, and a judge has just ended the CDC travel mask mandate, and some people are not happy. People will actually have a choice whether to wear a mask or not on planes, trains, and more. Imagine that choice after two and a half years! The DOJ will most likely try to appeal this because it is all about control, not science.

The cheers of passengers on planes were cool to see. The pandemic has hit a new phase, and we are going to have to live with it. **That's just the cold, hard truth!**

The problem has always been vultures taking advantage of the pain, but it will continue, unfortunately.

Misinformation and Disinformation 2022

IT'S JANUARY 14, 2022, and the president has come out talking about misinformation. Some networks are misleading the public and have to stop.

I think I can decide who is full of crap or not; that's the thing with freedom of thought. We can agree to disagree. What has happened during this pandemic is censorship of thought and discussion.

You have some doctors calling for JR to be censored for having Dr. RM on his show, talking about vaccines. These doctors have their own opinions, and that's okay, but to silence people who do not agree with you has been a problem.

It has cost lives, and to prove my point again, on January 19, 2022, a doctor from H Methodist was fired for saying that ivermectin helped patients. It kept them out of the hospital, which I thought was the purpose of early treatment.

I see it this way: if a therapeutic pill, vaccine, staying healthy, or losing weight keeps anyone out of the ICU or from dying, use it. Government forces should never have been an option in this country. America should have been that beacon of hope. Instead, it was a beacon of hate, anger and greed.

Who decides what is misinformation or truth?

It's January 24, 2022, and the CDC is starting to consider natural immunity as a positive thing but still wants everybody vaccinated. The FDA has also approved the use of Remdesivir for early treatment if needed.

The FDA has given its blessing for a drug that was being used in 2020 and 2021 by some doctors to treat COVID-19. It's 2022, and for some strange reason, it's only been given the green light now.

The FDA popped up on the radar in February 2022. Project Veritas captured video of FDA executive CC talking about annual COVID-19 shots and infant shots in the future. CC also brought up the fact that it's hard to get volunteers for testing, especially for pregnant women. So basically, the data pool is small; there are not enough test subjects. That explains why we are depending on other countries for the data.

So why do we have the FDA and CDC again?

Maybe the surgeon general can answer that question, or maybe not.

The US surgeon general, Dr. VM, is calling for censorship of misinformation. A difference of opinion is now misinformation, according to him. Like so many people before him, the JHC strikes again.

This time because JR talked about his COVID-19 treatment. JR did not push anybody to take the same treatment; he just discussed it on his podcast. Now people are calling for censoring JR, and celebs are leading the charge; even a US surgeon general is on board.

It's February 2022, and Surgeon General VM is on Capitol Hill talking about the mental health of the children. It's a little too late because the damage has already been done to the children of America.

Follow the science, we are following science, I represent science, they like to say.

Question to the reader: Who's most at risk from COVID-19?

On February 21, 2022, it was reported that the CDC had been holding back information. Their information is not ready for prime time, a spokesman for the CDC explains. So critical information that would benefit the people of this country is being withheld. It should make you wonder what this agency is doing.

Feeling Helpless and Sad

Depression and sadness are setting in more because most of our leaders give us little hope that we will be okay.

It will be a never-ending political agenda for vultures.

In the past, you had leaders who would inspire you and give these inspirational speeches of hope and strength.

Today, we have none of that.

It's all about power and greed.

It has become the pandemic of the greedy, the pandemic of the powerful.

To live, you must be vaccinated. We are in control, and we will come down on you if you don't. There is no choice in the land of the free; fuck the Constitution and the Bill of Rights. Let's not forget fuck your freedom. Come on, man!

That is the message; let's be honest about this. We are divided because that is what some people want in this country. The pandemic just gave them the green light to take more power and control.

Some people are okay with that, but once you give up your freedom, it is hard to get it back. History has shown us this time and time again, but to see this happening in America is heartbreaking.

People want to play God against the unknown, wanting to be in control of the uncontrollable. Two years in, and it seems like it's no longer about saving lives. Big pharma is making billions, and the CEO of Pfizer is planning for the fourth round of vaccines if he can get it cleared. Dr. Get Over It is still out making his rounds as it gets closer to 2022.

This story shows how far we have fallen into fear. On January 4, 2022, a mother puts her child in the trunk of her car because she does not want to catch COVID-19. She is taking him to a test site where the people there call the police, and she is booked into jail. She is also a teacher, which should scare the crap out of any parent out there.

The school places her on leave but really should let her go because this woman should not be around your kids.

If she could do this to her own child, I would hate to think what she could do to yours in school.

Then comes the LA writer who mocks the unvaccinated who have died. I will leave it there because he is not worth it!

On March 26, 2022, I catch this story on the local news. A family has lost four members of their family to the virus, and one needs a lung transplant. A double lung transplant to be exact because his lungs have so much damage.

To save a life someone must lose theirs. Heartbreaking all around.

As I write this journal, I have my ups and downs, as you can tell. I never thought in my lifetime that something like this would happen, but it did. It happened to all of us, so this really is your story. I am just the guy who wrote it down. What I saw and heard from different news outlets with a little opinion thrown in.

The sad thing is that some people had no self-reflection of the damage they caused. Ready to repeat their failures again!

Someone once said that we can learn from failure. Apparently, some people can't! History is filled with failures and successes. That is how life goes, but if things go bad and you repeat. Who is to blame in the end?

Lessons Learned?

Did the world learn anything from this nightmare? Some leaders did, and some did not! Mostly not by what I have been seeing.

What have I learned?

1. I learned that people are flawed; call it human nature, greed, or whatever! Some people are just fucked up! I am no saint, but these people make me look like a choir boy. Hate, greed, fear, and power destroyed the world. We were our own worst enemy; the bad orange man was gone, and that is all that mattered in the end. The resistance had won; we, the people, had lost, and we were going to keep on losing because hate destroys everything it touches.

2. People in power can be some of the most messed-up people in the world. The world has shown us that, country after country. Logic left the building, and it was all about power and control in the end. **A new world order, as some assholes have described it!**

3. Do your own research. Some doctors are better than others.

4. Here is an example: My friend has an eye disease called keratoconus, and for years he has dealt with it. He saw different doctors and finally found one who knew about his condition. An expert that helped him see okay, but this eye disease progresses over time. It calls for an eye transplant in the end to see.

Not a great option, but he's not there yet.

A few years later, he watched the Winter Games and the night train bobsled team. The captain of the team has the same condition, and he researches the doctor who helped Holcomb see better. It looks like he might have found a doctor who can make his vision more stable—no transplant. My friend goes to his eye doctor and tells him about the procedure, but his doctor blows it off as nonsense.

So my friend holds out for a few more years until his doctor says no more can be done. So he decides to go for it. He has done his research and has all the information. So the call is made.

Today, his vision is stable, but he wishes he had done the operation sooner.

All doctors are not created equal; some innovate and grow. Train in new procedures and techniques. Some just stay in one place and do the bare minimum. Some doctors have better skill levels than others.

Remember, there is a show called Botched for a reason!

5. The mainstream and social media suck. I watched to compare stories. It was night and day in coverage. Fear vs. Freedom: Darkness vs. Light. Talk about vultures!

6. To appreciate the people, I love and care about them more because we are not guaranteed tomorrow.

Nope on Review 2022

It's October 21, 2022, and I am back to see if any vultures did an after-action review or had any self-reflection moments! Big surprise, no one did!

California is going to punish doctors if they talk about COVID-19 in a way that does not toe the government line. **The Misinformation Police!** A doctor can lose their license just for doing their job. **Thanks, GN and the Sacramento vultures. It is an actual law, signed and sealed.**

Not to be outdone, it was reported that a Boston university is messing around with the Omicron variant and the original virus. A deadly combination with an 80 percent death ratio. The university denies the report, but with most of the health experts failing in their decision-making and flip-flopping so much, the story is probably true. It would not be a surprise to me, after the hell the world has gone through, that the experts would try to keep the monster alive and make it more deadly.

The CDC has also jumped in and recommended a vaccine for your kids to attend school. Let's be honest; it's a mandate. No vaccine, no school for your child.

The people in charge have learned nothing from their mistakes. They will keep making things worse because they can't help themselves, and all of us will pay the price in the end.

When I started writing this journal in 2020, it was to tell the story of people and a pandemic that would change the world.

Fifteen days, we were told, and look where we are today. **Going into 2023!**

A nurse once said it was like chasing the devil. Death surrounded her in a nursing home, and there was little she could do about it. That was at the beginning of this nightmare.

Hate, fear, anger, lies, and destruction, that stuff is easy. It's love, peace, forgiveness, understanding, and truth that are hard.

Imagine if it had been a total team effort, without all the hate. Some lives could have been saved, but that's not what happened. Let's be honest: in 2023, no one was going to stop the virus, and the vaccines did not stop the transmission. That is the truth, period!

It's not misinformation; it's a fact!

The sad thing is that it's January 23, 2023, now, and the vultures are still making people suffer. I guess some people love misery.

So I will end this journal with a final entry to remember the people we have lost and for those who survived.

To the people of America and around the world.

We have lived through a difficult time in history. Millions of lives have been lost, but they will never be forgotten as long as they remain in our hearts. We will remember the times we spent with our loved ones and the happiness they brought to our lives. Their spirit and love will carry on inside us because these things can never die. We will see our loved ones some day in a world that is beyond belief. Where there is peace, but most of all, love. Our hearts are broken, but our spirits must stay strong because we will continue our journey in life until we are called home. Until that day comes, hold onto the ones you love a little tighter, don't sweat the small stuff in life, and live life to the fullest. Enjoy what God has given you because it's all around you; all you have to do is slow down and look. It's your family, friends, and the love you have for one another. It is a blue sky, a star-filled night, a snow-capped mountain, or a calm sea. My hope and prayer is that we never go through something like this again. God bless all of you.

About the Author

This is my first journal, and it deals with the **history** of COVID-19. My story is like many in the world: a struggle to survive the unknown. I lost my mother five weeks into the lockdowns—I did not lose her to the virus but to dementia.

I stayed away because of the lockdowns and talked to her on the phone, but her condition worsened. She had stopped eating and drinking. I was told that her kidneys were shutting down. The staff did the best they could, but this was the final stage of the disease she had struggled with for years. She held on for a while, but with the lockdowns in place, I could not help her. All I could do was visit her through a closed window until her final day. On that day, I was allowed in to say goodbye to my hero.

I wanted to share my story with the readers.

This pandemic broke the world and, along with it, many hearts.